Using the number line: Counting in ones

```
← • • • • • • • • • • • • • • • • • • • • •
  0 1 2 3 4 5 6 7 8 9 10 11 12 13 14 15 16 17 18 19 20
```

A Write the number that is

one more than 3 ___4___   one more than 10 _____

one more than 4 _____   one more than 14 _____

one more than 6 _____   one more than 17 _____

one more than 7 _____   one more than 19 _____

one more than 9 _____   one more than 16 _____

B Write the number that is

one less than 2 _____   one less than 14 _____

one less than 4 _____   one less than 15 _____

one less than 7 _____   one less than 17 _____

one less than 10 _____   one less than 18 _____

one less than 12 _____   one less than 20 _____

C Finish these

2 is one more than _____   12 is one more than _____

9 is one more than _____   16 is one more than _____

4 is one more than _____   10 is one more than _____

7 is one more than _____   18 is one more than _____

5 is one more than _____   20 is one more than _____

4 is one less than _____   13 is one less than _____

1 is one less than _____   15 is one less than _____

6 is one less than _____   19 is one less than _____

9 is one less than _____   11 is one less than _____

3 is one less than _____   17 is one less than _____

2   Tick the shapes that have one quarter shaded.

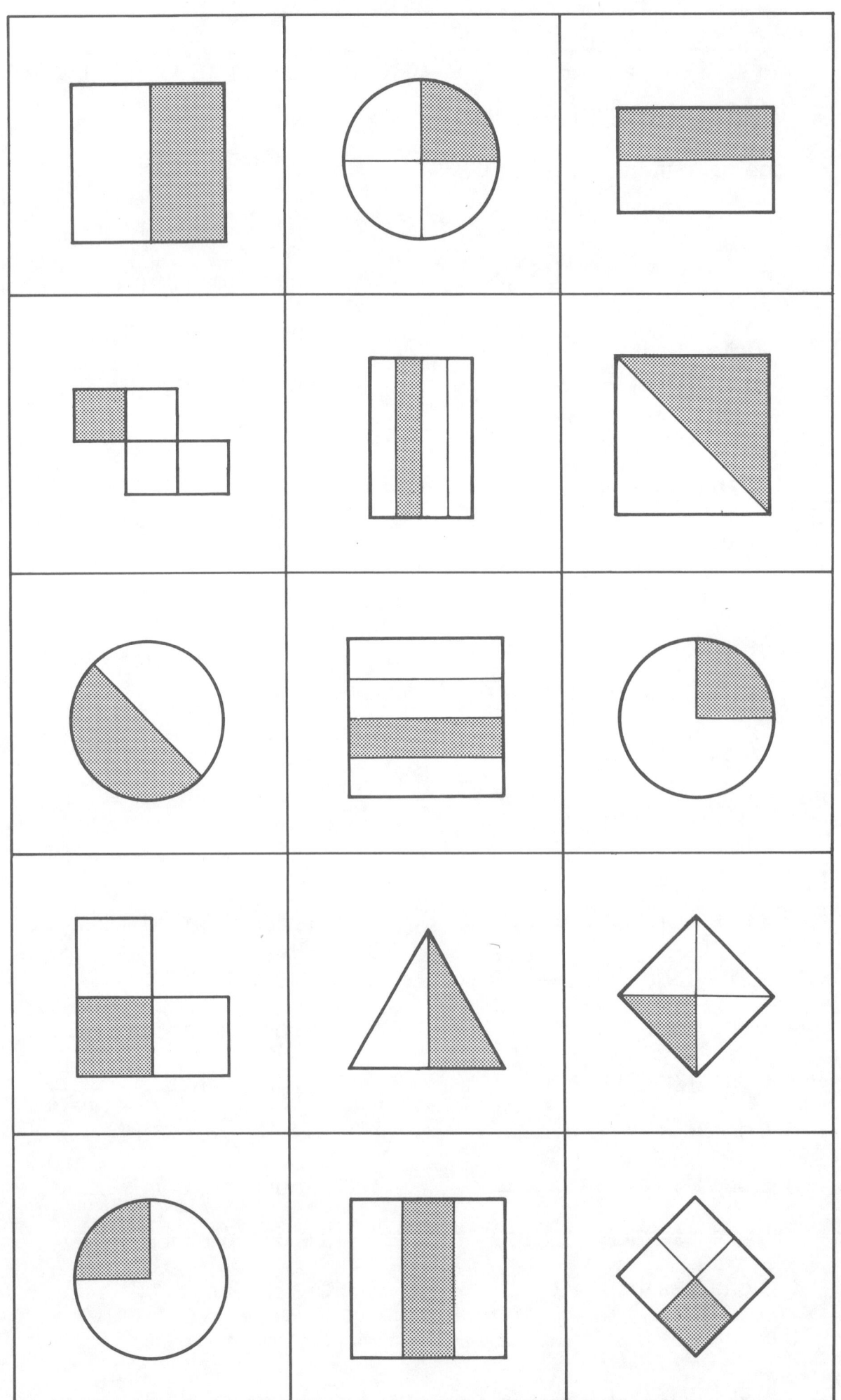

Shade one quarter of each shape. 3

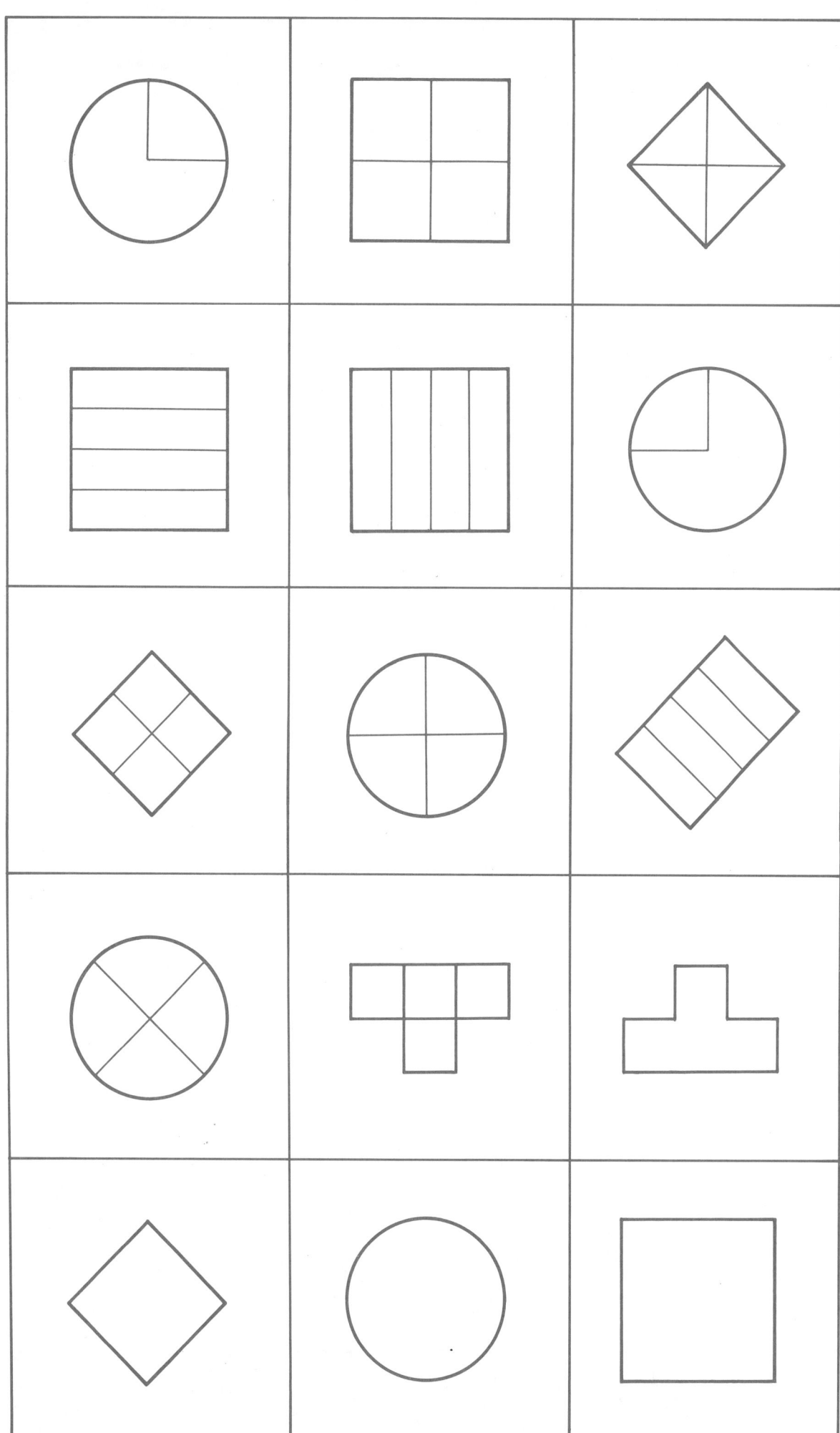

4 What time is it?

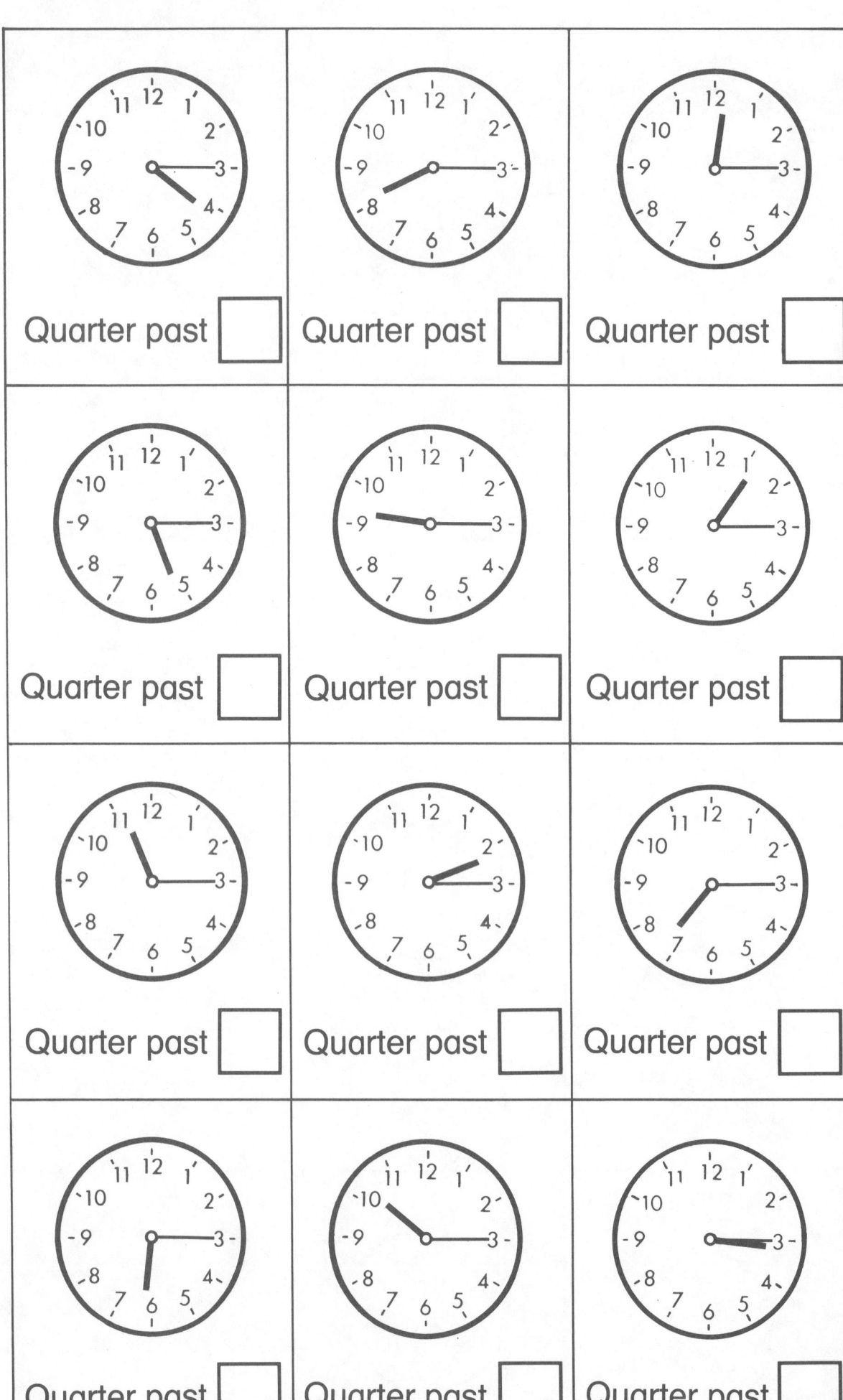

Quarter past ☐   Quarter past ☐   Quarter past ☐

Quarter past ☐   Quarter past ☐   Quarter past ☐

Quarter past ☐   Quarter past ☐   Quarter past ☐

Quarter past ☐   Quarter past ☐   Quarter past ☐

What time is it? 5

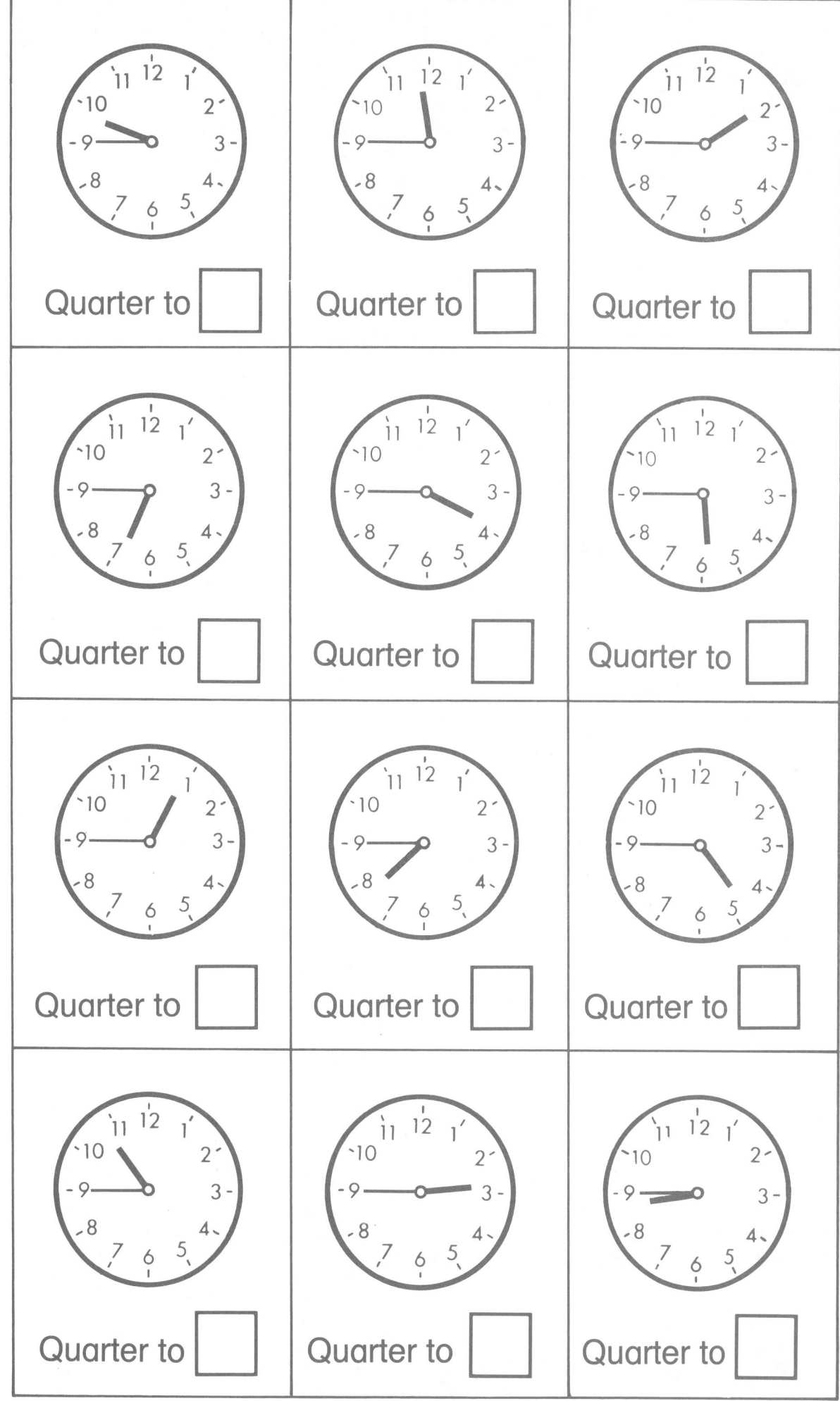

6   Using the number line: Counting on.
    Finish the number sentences.

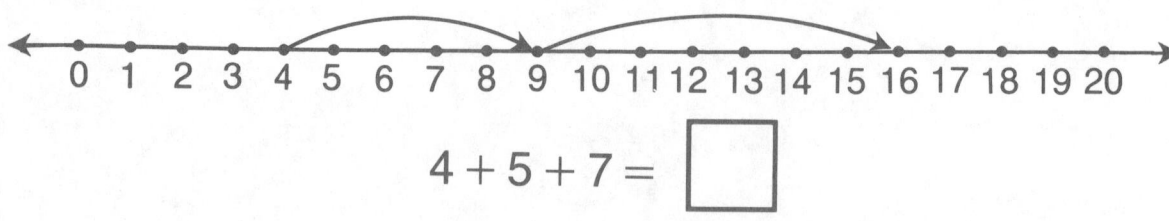

$4 + 5 + 7 = \boxed{}$

$4 + 7 + 5 = \boxed{}$

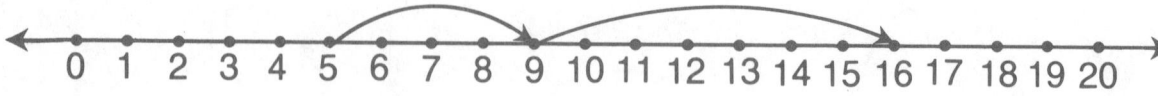

$5 + 7 + 4 = \boxed{}$

$5 + 4 + 7 = \boxed{}$

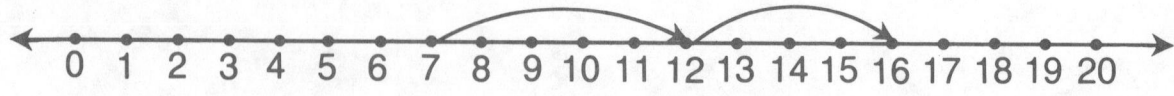

$7 + 4 + 5 = \boxed{}$

$7 + 5 + 4 = \boxed{}$

Using the number line: Counting on. 7
Show the steps on the number line.
Finish the number sentences.

5 + 6 + 8 = ☐

5 + 8 + 6 = ☐

6 + 8 + 5 = ☐

6 + 5 + 8 = ☐

8 + 5 + 6 = ☐

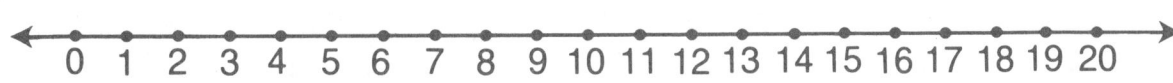

8 + 6 + 5 = ☐

8 Using the number line: Counting on.
Finish the number sentences.

```
← • • • • • • • • • • • • • • • • • • • • • →
  0 1 2 3 4 5 6 7 8 9 10 11 12 13 14 15 16 17 18 19 20
```

3 + 4 + 8 = ☐   4 + 3 + 8 = ☐

3 + 8 + 4 = ☐   8 + 3 + 4 = ☐

4 + 8 + 3 = ☐   8 + 4 + 3 = ☐

1 + 3 + 9 = ☐   3 + 1 + 9 = ☐

1 + 9 + 3 = ☐   9 + 1 + 3 = ☐

3 + 9 + 1 = ☐   9 + 3 + 1 = ☐

2 + 8 + 10 = ☐   8 + 2 + 10 = ☐

2 + 10 + 8 = ☐   10 + 2 + 8 = ☐

8 + 10 + 2 = ☐   10 + 8 + 2 = ☐

3 + 6 + 9 = ☐   6 + 3 + 9 = ☐

3 + 9 + 6 = ☐   9 + 3 + 6 = ☐

6 + 9 + 3 = ☐   9 + 6 + 3 = ☐

1 + 2 + 8 = ☐   2 + 1 + 8 = ☐

1 + 8 + 2 = ☐   8 + 1 + 2 = ☐

2 + 8 + 1 = ☐   8 + 2 + 1 = ☐

Using the number line: Counting on.
Finish the number sentences.

3 + 6 + 7 = ☐   6 + 3 + 7 = ☐
3 + 7 + 6 = ☐   7 + 3 + 6 = ☐
6 + 7 + 3 = ☐   7 + 6 + 3 = ☐

1 + 4 + 9 = ☐   4 + 1 + 9 = ☐
1 + 9 + 4 = ☐   9 + 1 + 4 = ☐
4 + 9 + 1 = ☐   9 + 4 + 1 = ☐

2 + 5 + 10 = ☐   5 + 2 + 10 = ☐
2 + 10 + 5 = ☐   10 + 2 + 5 = ☐
5 + 10 + 2 = ☐   10 + 5 + 2 = ☐

4 + 7 + 9 = ☐   7 + 4 + 9 = ☐
4 + 9 + 7 = ☐   9 + 4 + 7 = ☐
7 + 9 + 4 = ☐   9 + 7 + 4 = ☐

2 + 4 + 6 = ☐   4 + 2 + 6 = ☐
2 + 6 + 4 = ☐   6 + 2 + 4 = ☐
4 + 6 + 2 = ☐   6 + 4 + 2 = ☐

10 Using the number line: Counting in twos.

0 2 4 6 8 10 12 14 16 18 20 22 24 26 28 30

2+2=☐   6+2=☐   8+2=☐   16+2=☐

18+2=☐   24+2=☐   26+2=☐   28+2=☐

2−2=☐   4−2=☐   10−2=☐   14−2=☐

18−2=☐   22−2=☐   24−2=☐   30−2=☐

4	8	12	14	18	22	24	28
+2	+2	+2	+2	+2	+2	+2	+2
___	___	____	____	____	____	____	____

2	6	8	10	16	20	26	28
−2	−2	−2	−2	−2	−2	−2	−2
___	___	___	____	____	____	____	____

Which number is

2 greater than 8? ☐   2 greater than 14? ☐

2 greater than 24? ☐   2 greater than 28? ☐

2 greater than 10? ☐   2 greater than 20? ☐

2 less than 26? ☐   2 less than 10? ☐

2 less than 22? ☐   2 less than 6? ☐

2 less than 18? ☐   2 less than 12? ☐

Count on in twos from 8 ___ ___ ___ ___ ___ ___

Count back in twos from 18 ___ ___ ___ ___ ___ ___

Write the missing numerals.   11

2 4 6 8 ◇ 12 14 16

4 6 ◇ 10 12 14 ◇ 18

8 10 12 ◇ 16 ◇ 20 ◇

12 14 ◇ 18 20 22 ◇ ◇

◇ 18 20 ◇ 24 26 28 ◇

20 18 16 14 ◇ 10 8 6

24 22 20 ◇ 16 14 ◇ 10

28 ◇ ◇ 22 20 18 16 14

◇ 14 12 10 ◇ 6 4 ◇

18 16 ◇ ◇ 10 8 ◇ 4

12   Making numbers up to the next ten.

Make these numbers up to 10.

5 + ☐ = 10

6 + ☐ = 10

7 + ☐ = 10

8 + ☐ = 10

9 + ☐ = 10

Make these numbers up to 20.

14 + ☐ = 20   17 + ☐ = 20

15 + ☐ = 20   18 + ☐ = 20

16 + ☐ = 20   19 + ☐ = 20

Making numbers up to the next ten.

Make these numbers up to 30.

27 + ☐ = 30   29 + ☐ = 30

21 + ☐ = 30   22 + ☐ = 30

25 + ☐ = 30   28 + ☐ = 30

23 + ☐ = 30   26 + ☐ = 30

Make these numbers up to 40.

34 + ☐ = 40   35 + ☐ = 40

38 + ☐ = 40   31 + ☐ = 40

32 + ☐ = 40   37 + ☐ = 40

39 + ☐ = 40   33 + ☐ = 40

Make these numbers up to 50.

44 + ☐ = 50   43 + ☐ = 50

46 + ☐ = 50   47 + ☐ = 50

49 + ☐ = 50   48 + ☐ = 50

41 + ☐ = 50   42 + ☐ = 50

14   Length: Measure each line in centimetres (cm).

7 cm

Length: Draw the lines. 15

Draw a line 6 cm long.

Draw a line 11 cm long.

Draw a line 8 cm long.

Draw a line 3 cm long.

Draw a line 13 cm long.

Draw a line 10 cm long.

Draw a line 7 cm long.

Draw a line 4 cm long.

Draw a line 1 cm long.

Draw a line 2 cm long.

Draw a line 12 cm long.

Draw a line 9 cm long.

Draw a line 5 cm long.

Draw a line 14 cm long.

16 Addition:
Work from left to right.

2	12	12	
+4	+4	+14	12 + 14 =
—	—	—	

3	13	13	
+5	+5	+15	13 + 15 =
—	—	—	

6	16	16	
+2	+2	+12	16 + 12 =
—	—	—	

7	17	17	
+1	+1	+11	17 + 11 =
—	—	—	

2	12	12	
+7	+7	+17	12 + 17 =
—	—	—	

4	14	14	
+1	+1	+11	14 + 11 =
—	—	—	

3	13	13	
+4	+4	+14	13 + 14 =
—	—	—	

4	14	14	
+5	+5	+15	14 + 15 =
—	—	—	

2	12	12	
+2	+2	+12	12 + 12 =
—	—	—	

Subtraction:
Write the number sentences and the answers.

Jane had 26 pence.   She spent 14 pence.   How much was left?

$26p - 14p = 12p$ Answer:

Tom had 28 pence. He spent 15 pence. How much was left?

Answer:

Sally had 28 pence. She spent 12 pence. How much was left?

Answer:

How much more is 28 pence than 11 pence?

$28p - 11p =$ Answer:

How much more is 29 pence than 17 pence?

Answer:

How much more is 25 pence than 11 pence?

Answer:

What must be added to 14 pence to make 27 pence?

$27p - 14p =$ Answer:

What must be added to 15 pence to make 29 pence?

Answer:

What must be added to 12 pence to make 24 pence?

Answer:

18 Counting in fives.

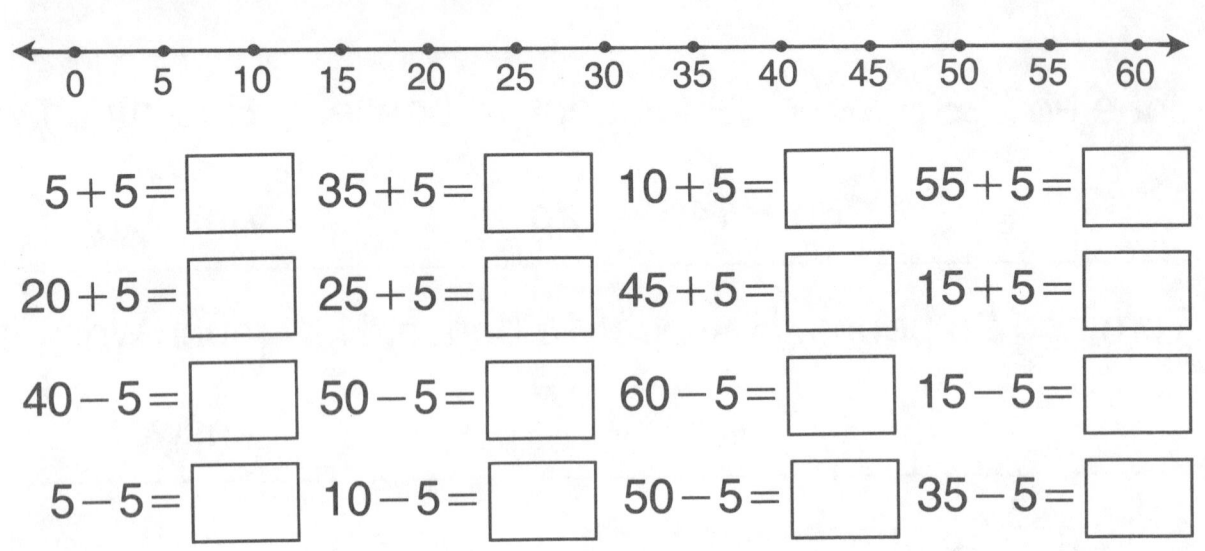

Fill in the empty labels round the clock face with these details:

5 minutes to   10 minutes past
quarter to   quarter past
20 minutes to   25 minutes past
         half past

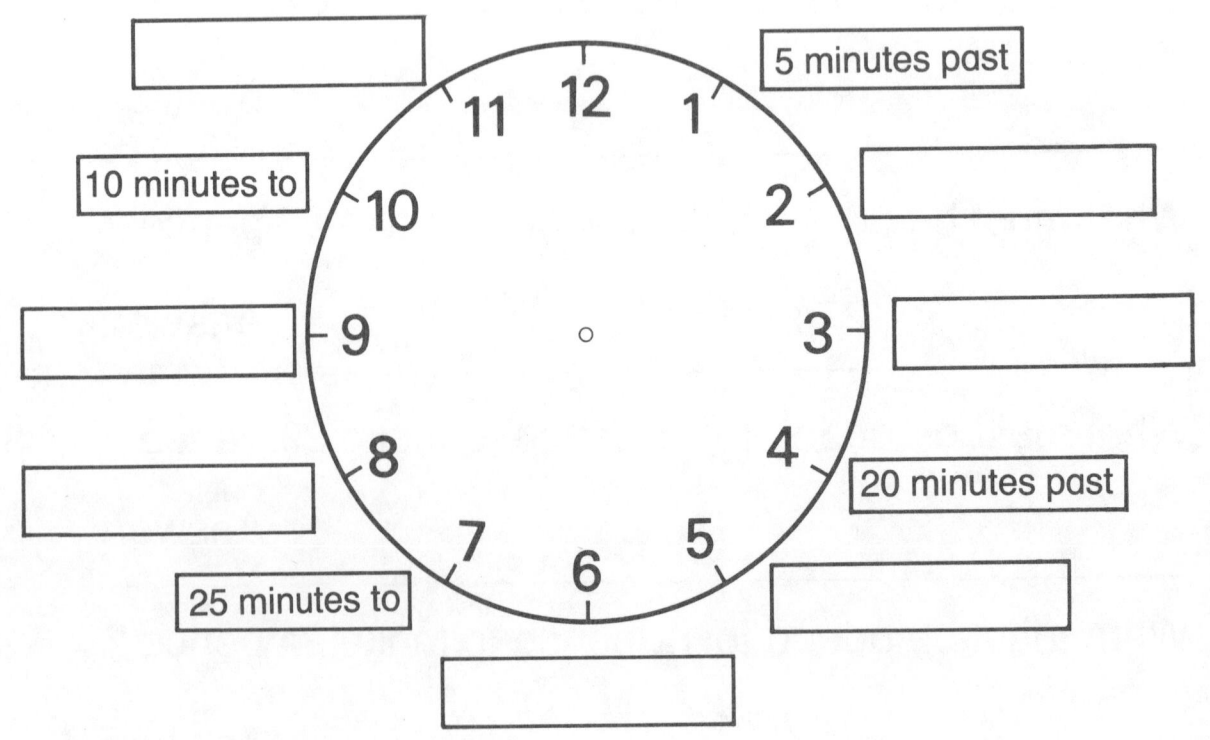

Write the missing numerals.

5 10 15 20 25 ◇ 35 40

20 25 30 ◇ 40 45 ◇ 55

◇ 30 35 40 45 50 55 ◇

15 20 ◇ 30 ◇ 40 ◇ 50

◇ ◇ 15 20 25 30 35 ◇

50 45 40 35 30 25 ◇ 15

◇ 50 ◇ 40 35 30 25 20

40 35 30 25 20 ◇ 10 ◇

60 ◇ 50 ◇ ◇ 35 30 25

45 ◇ 35 ◇ 25 ◇ 15 ◇

20   Counting in tens.

```
 ←———•———•———•———•———•———•———•———•———•———•———→
     0   10  20  30  40  50  60  70  80  90  100
```

10+10= ☐   50+10= ☐   80+10= ☐   20+10= ☐
40+10= ☐   90+10= ☐   60+10= ☐   30+10= ☐
50−10= ☐   90−10= ☐   20−10= ☐   70−10= ☐
40−10= ☐   80−10= ☐   100−10= ☐   30−10= ☐

Complete the following:

10 or ten means   <u>one ten</u>

20 or twenty means   <u>two tens</u>

30 or thirty means   _____

40 or forty means   _____

50 or fifty means   _____

60 or sixty means   _____

70 or seventy means   _____

80 or eighty means   _____

90 or ninety means   _____

100 or one hundred means _____

Write the numeral that is:

10 more than 70 ☐   10 less than 60 ☐

Draw a ring round the answer. 21

40 =	10 + 4	(30 + 10)	30 − 10	60 − 10
70 =	90 − 10	60 + 1	80 − 10	7 + 10
50 =	60 − 10	5 + 10	30 + 2	70 − 10
10 =	1 + 10	90 − 8	10 + 10	20 − 10
60 =	50 + 10	50 − 10	30 + 3	6 + 10
80 =	70 + 1	8 + 0	70 − 10	10 + 70
30 =	50 + 20	40 − 10	80 − 5	3 + 10
90 =	9 + 10	80 + 1	100 − 10	100 − 1
100 =	90 + 10	90 − 10	10 + 10	10 + 0
20 =	2 + 10	30 − 10	40 + 20	40 − 10
60 =	70 − 10	6 + 10	80 − 10	40 + 2
80 =	8 + 10	70 − 10	50 + 3	70 + 10
30 =	20 − 10	50 − 10	10 + 20	3 + 10
50 =	5 + 10	40 − 1	30 + 40	40 + 10
100 =	1 + 20	10 + 90	90 − 10	50 + 5

22   Using the number line: Counting on in tens.
     Finish the number sentences.

40 + 20 = ☐

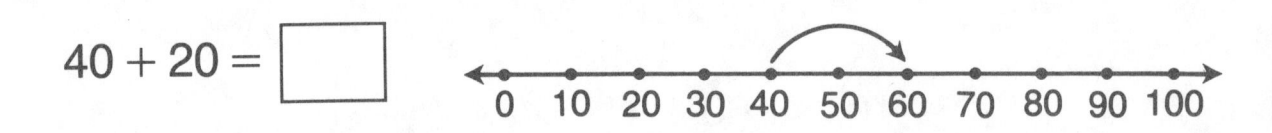

10 + 30 = ☐

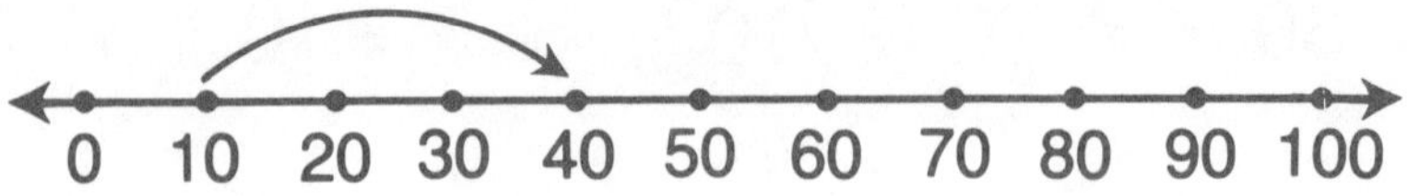

40 + 40 = ☐

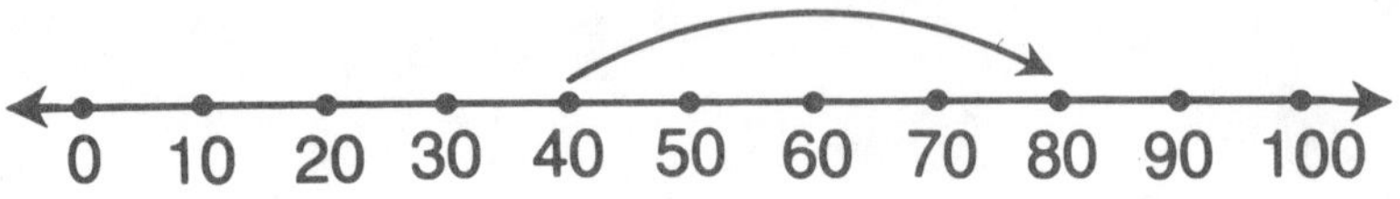

30 + 20 = ☐

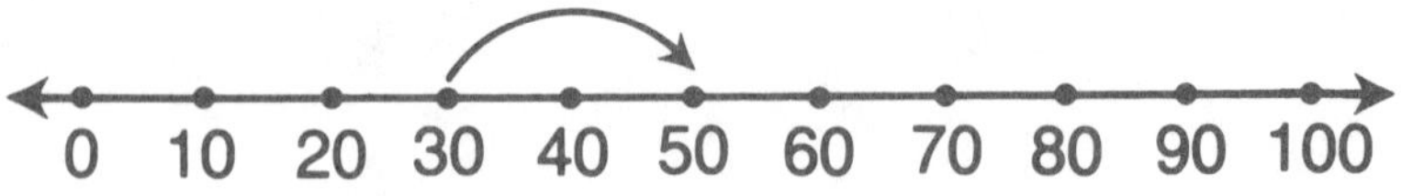

20 + 50 = ☐

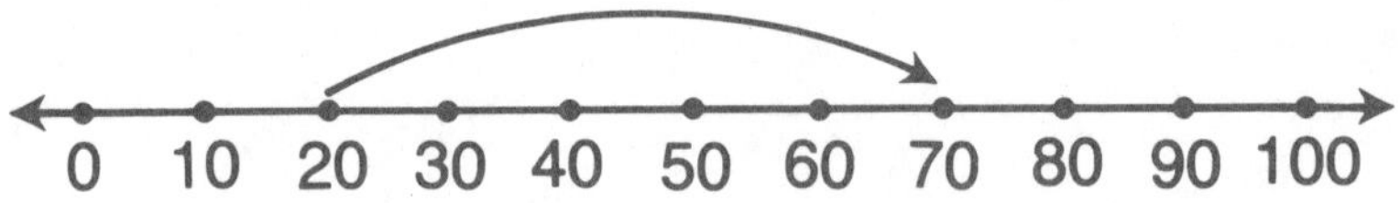

70 + 30 = ☐

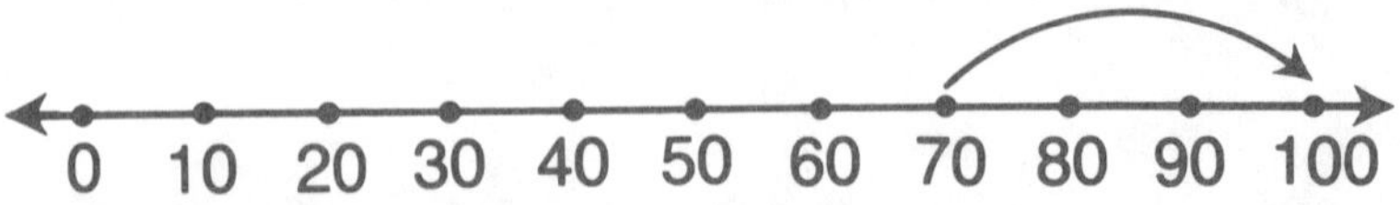

30 + 60 = ☐

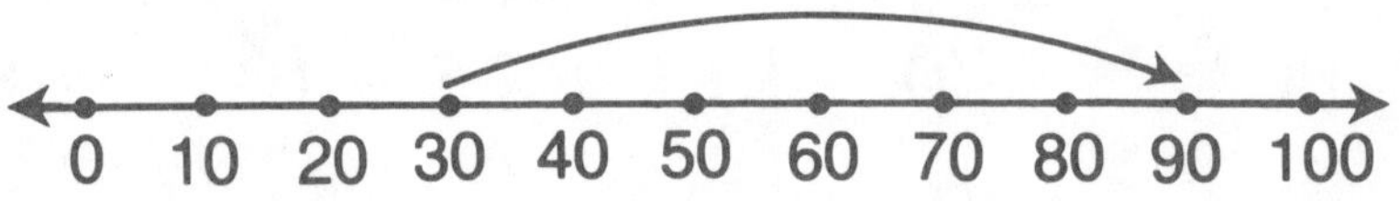

20 + 40 = ☐

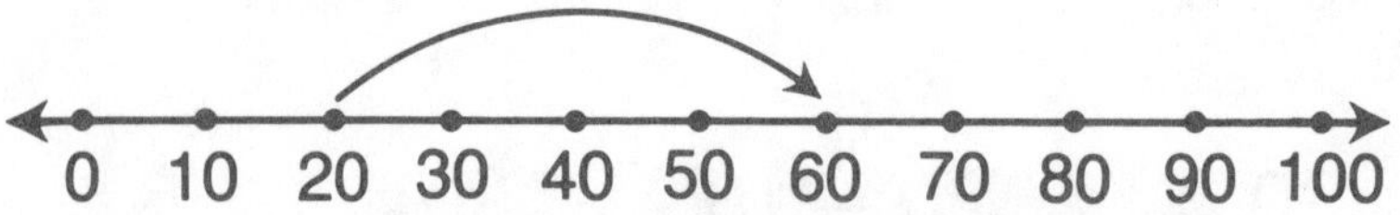

30 + 50 = ☐

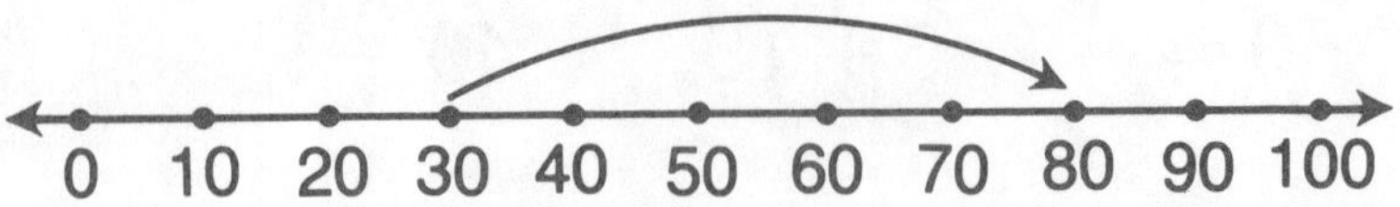

Using the number line: Counting on in tens. 23
Show the steps on the number line.
Finish the number sentences.

40 + 30 = ☐

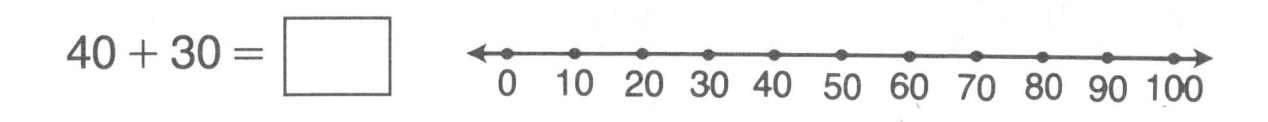

10 + 20 = ☐

50 + 40 = ☐

50 + 50 = ☐

10 + 40 = ☐

60 + 10 = ☐

30 + 30 = ☐

20 + 20 = ☐

60 + 40 = ☐

24 Using the number line: Counting back in tens.
Finish the number sentences.

60 − 30 = ☐

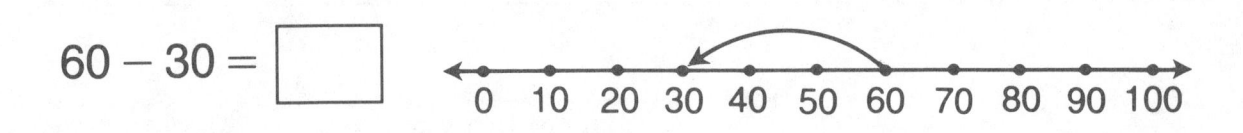

70 − 50 = ☐

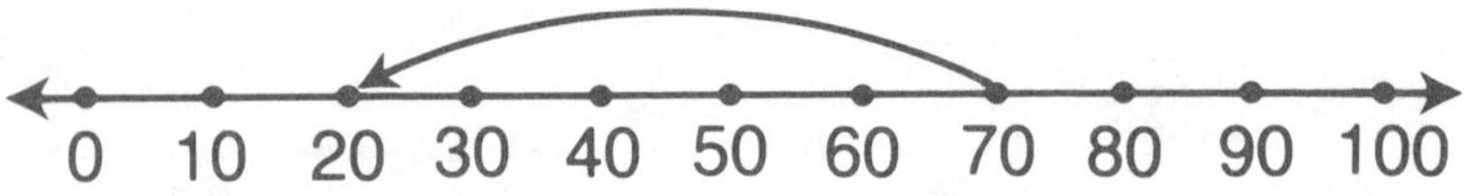

100 − 20 = ☐

50 − 40 = ☐

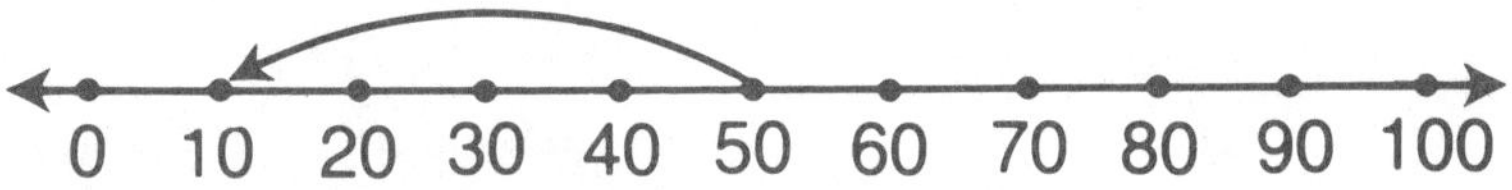

100 − 60 = ☐

90 − 50 = ☐

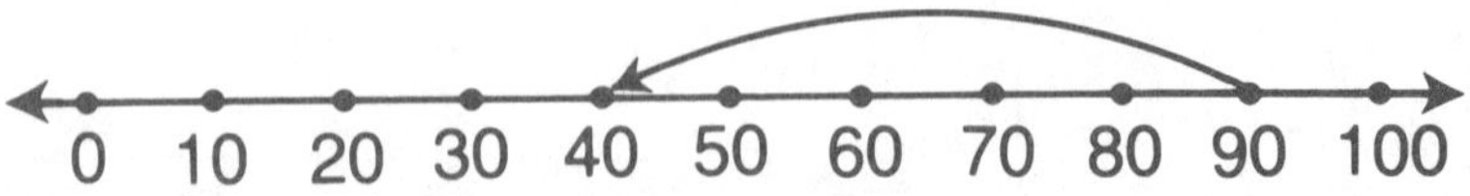

70 − 40 = ☐

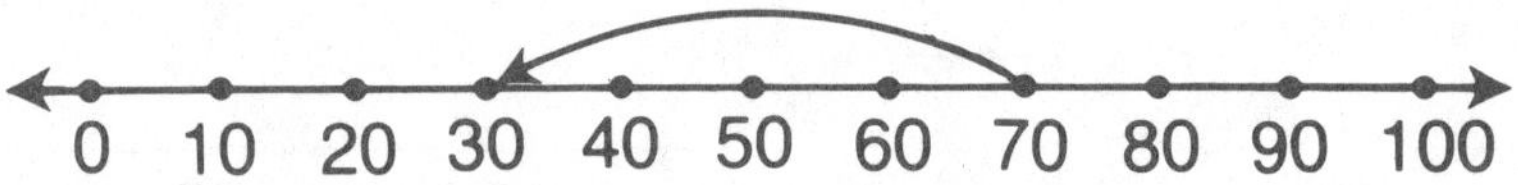

80 − 30 = ☐

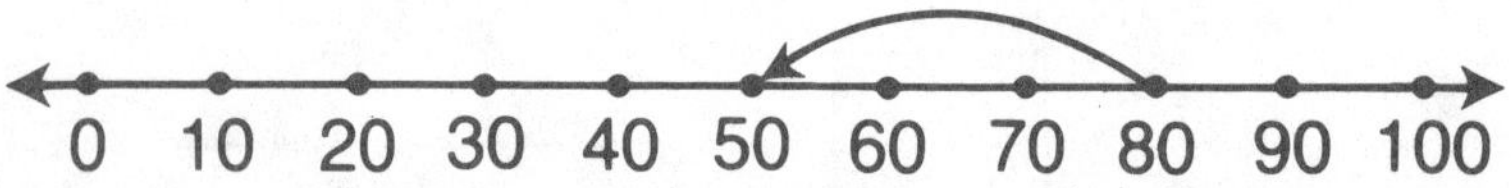

70 − 60 = ☐

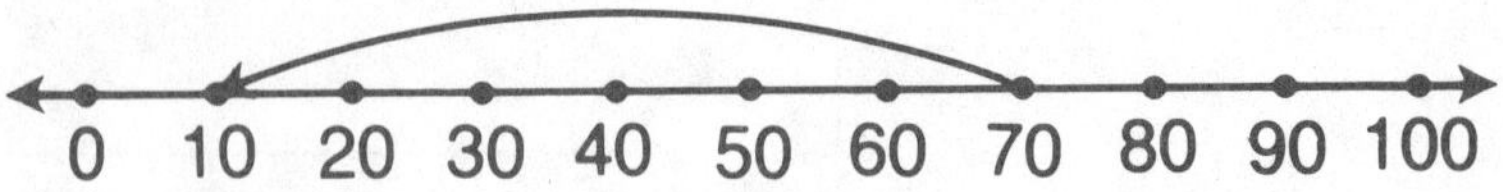

Using the number line: Counting back in tens.
Show the steps on the number line.
Finish the number sentences.

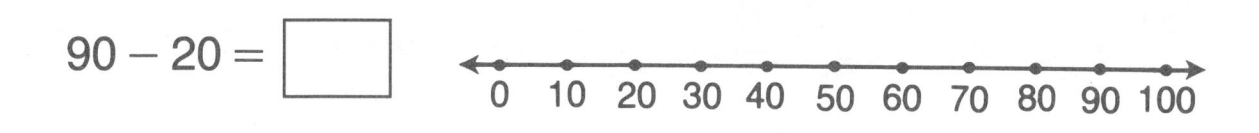

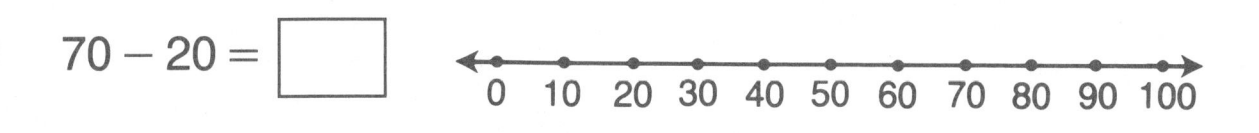

90 − 20 = ☐

50 − 30 = ☐

100 − 10 = ☐

70 − 20 = ☐

100 − 40 = ☐

90 − 30 = ☐

80 − 50 = ☐

100 − 20 = ☐

90 − 40 = ☐

26. Add the coins. How many pence?

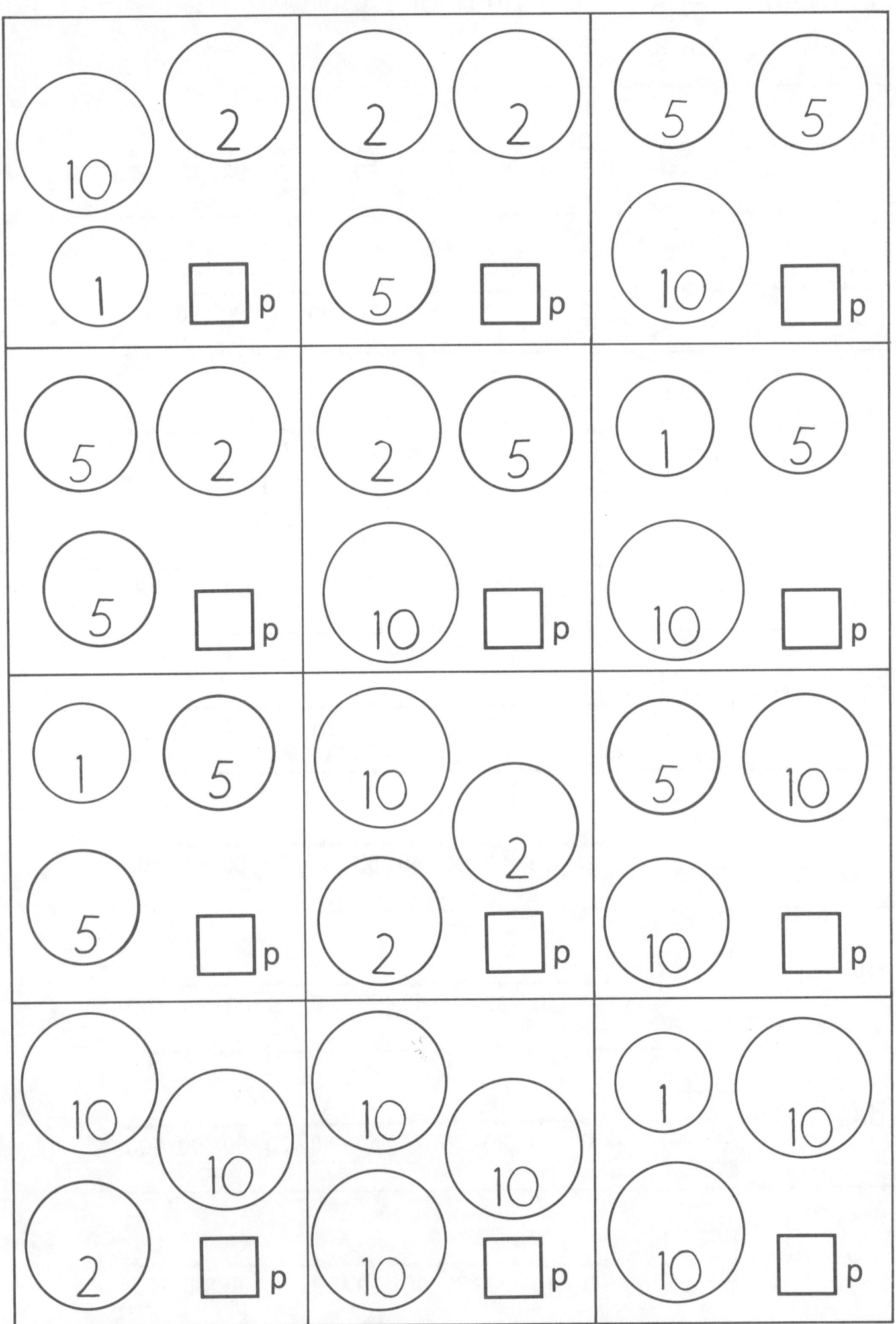

Add the coins. How many pence? 27

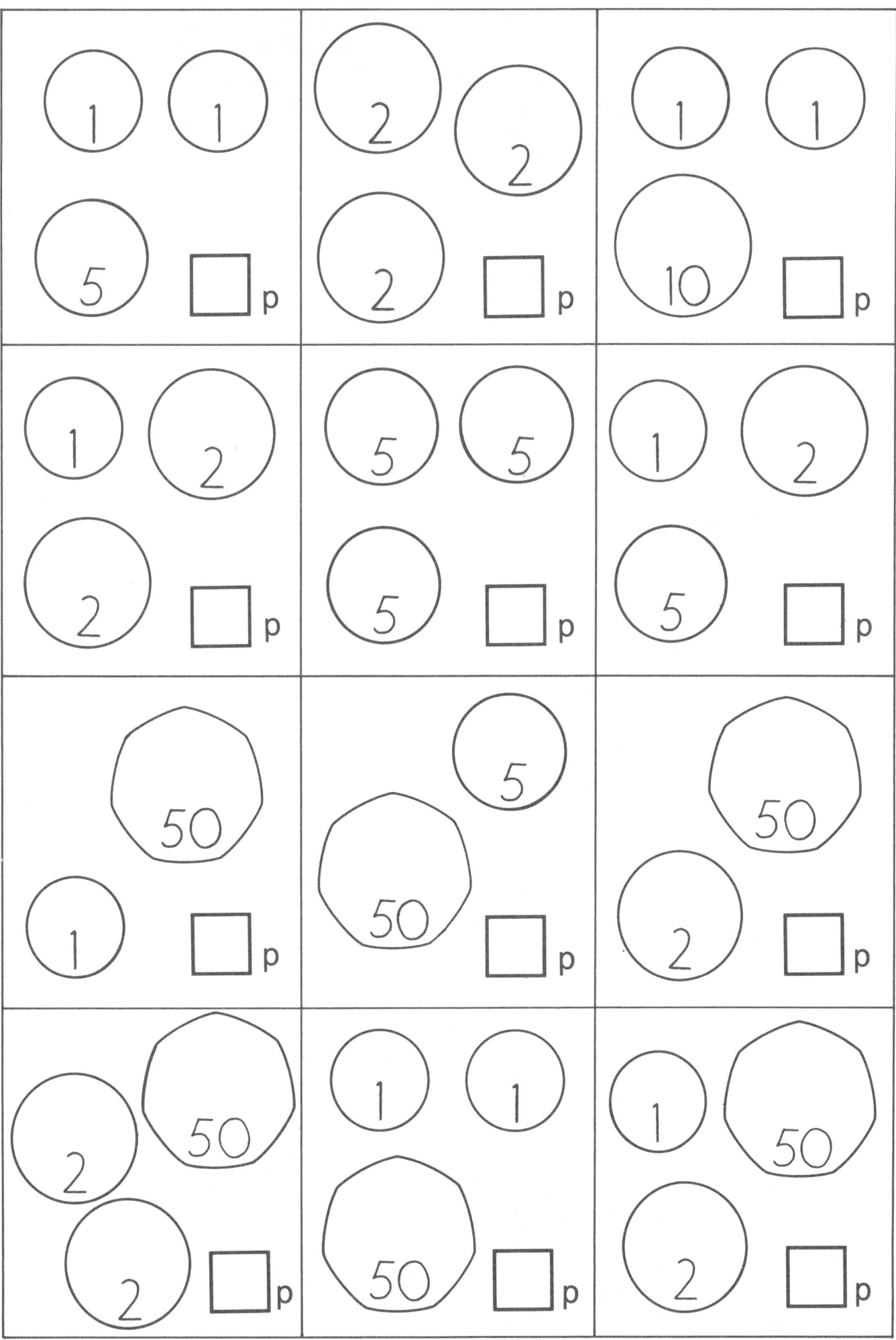

28 Addition:
Work from left to right.

2	32	32	
+3	+3	+13	32 + 13 =
—	—	—	

4	34	34	
+2	+2	+32	34 + 32 =
—	—	—	

1	61	61	
+4	+4	+24	61 + 24 =
—	—	—	

5	45	45	
+2	+2	+12	45 + 12 =
—	—	—	

6	46	46	
+3	+3	+33	46 + 33 =
—	—	—	

6	76	76	
+2	+2	+22	76 + 22 =
—	—	—	

4	44	44	
+3	+3	+23	44 + 23 =
—	—	—	

4	64	64	
+5	+5	+25	64 + 25 =
—	—	—	

7	47	47	
+2	+2	+12	47 + 12 =
—	—	—	

Subtraction:

Write the number sentences and the answers.

Andrew had 45 pence. He spent 13 pence. How much was left?

    45p − 13p = 32p   Answer:

Judith had 66 pence. She spent 32 pence. How much was left?

     Answer:

Martin had 85 pence. He spent 24 pence. How much was left?

     Answer:

How much more is 57 pence than 12 pence?

    57p − 12p =   Answer:

How much more is 79 pence than 33 pence?

     Answer:

How much more is 98 pence than 22 pence?

     Answer:

What must be added to 23 pence to make 67 pence?

    67p − 23p =   Answer:

What must be added to 25 pence to make 89 pence?

     Answer:

What must be added to 12 pence to make 59 pence?

     Answer:

30 Numbers above one hundred.

Write these numbers in words. The first two are done for you.

101 <u>one hundred and one</u>
102 <u>one hundred and two</u>
103 _____
104 _____
105 _____
106 _____
107 _____
108 _____
109 _____
110 _____

Write these numbers in figures. The first two are done for you.

one hundred and twelve	<u>112</u>
one hundred and sixteen	<u>116</u>
one hundred and twenty eight	_____
one hundred and thirty five	_____
one hundred and forty three	_____
one hundred and fifty nine	_____
one hundred and sixty one	_____
one hundred and seventy six	_____
one hundred and eighty four	_____
one hundred and ninety seven	_____

Write in figures the number shown on each abacus:

100	10	1
•	••	••
	•	••
		•

100	10	1
•	•	

100	10	1
•		••
		••
		•

_____   _____   _____

Numbers above one hundred.   31

160 + 10 = ☐   140 + 10 = ☐   120 + 10 = ☐

110 + 10 = ☐   100 + 10 = ☐   180 + 10 = ☐

130 + 10 = ☐   170 + 10 = ☐   150 + 10 = ☐

150 − 10 = ☐   110 − 10 = ☐   180 − 10 = ☐

120 − 10 = ☐   190 − 10 = ☐   130 − 10 = ☐

170 − 10 = ☐   140 − 10 = ☐   160 − 10 = ☐

Write these numbers in figures:

one hundred and twenty ——   one hundred and seventy ——
one hundred and fifty   ——   one hundred and forty   ——
one hundred and eighty ——   one hundred and ninety   ——
one hundred and thirty ——   one hundred and ten   ——

Count on in tens from 100 to 160:

100 ——   ——   ——   ——   ——   160

Count back in tens from 200 to 140:

200 ——   ——   ——   ——   ——   140

Write in figures the number shown on each abacus:

100	10	1
•	••••• •••	

100	10	1
••		

100	10	1
•	••••	

____   ____   ____

32. Using the number line: Counting on in tens.
Show the steps on the number line.
Finish the number sentences.

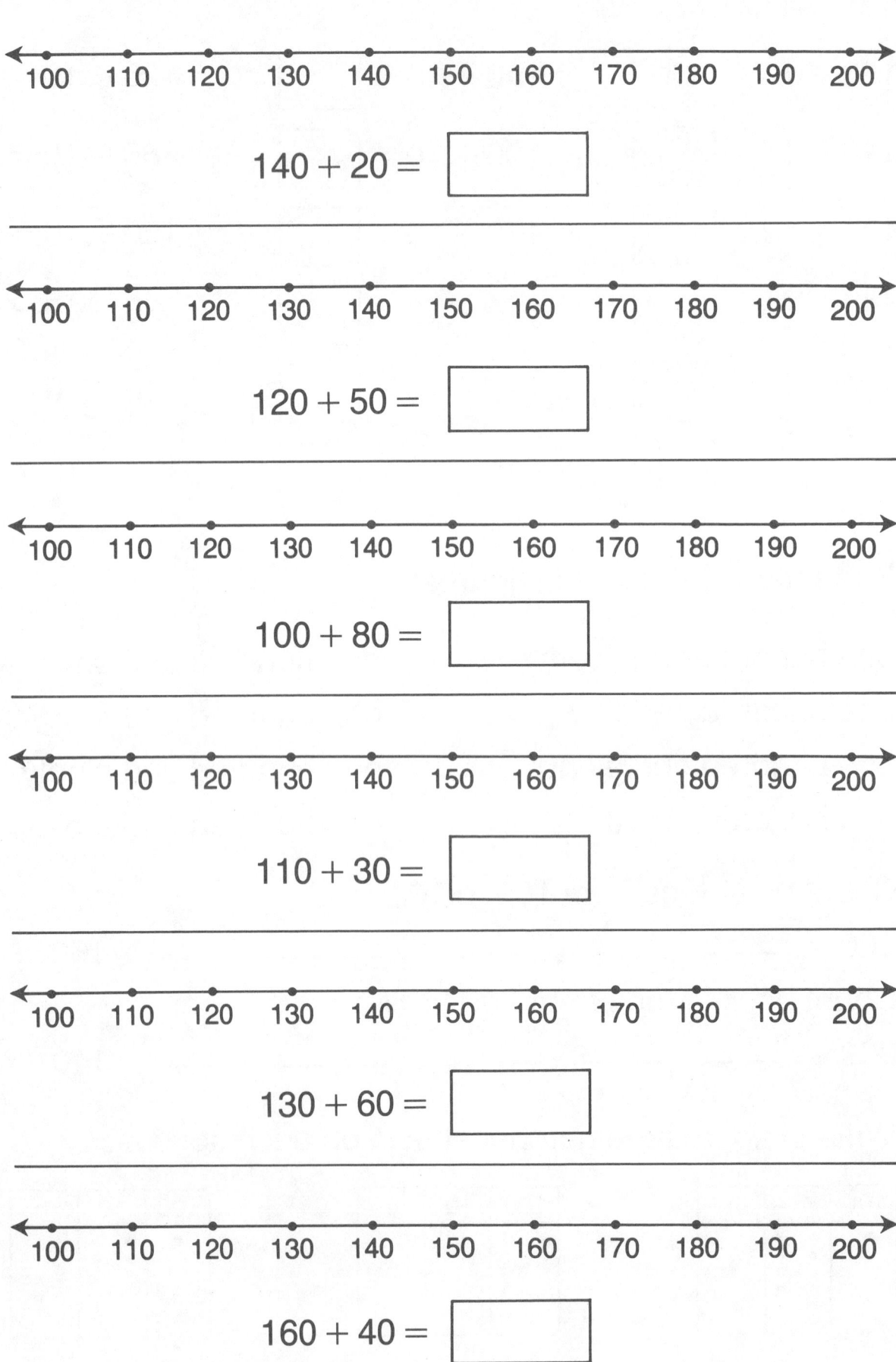

140 + 20 =

120 + 50 =

100 + 80 =

110 + 30 =

130 + 60 =

160 + 40 =

Using the number line: Counting back in tens. 33
Show the steps on the number line.
Finish the number sentences.

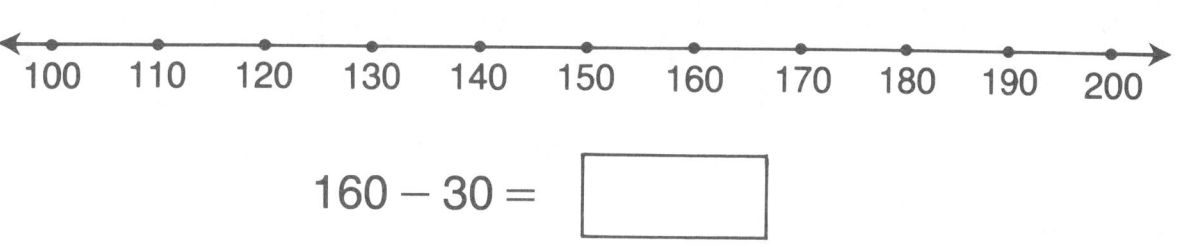

160 − 30 = [130]

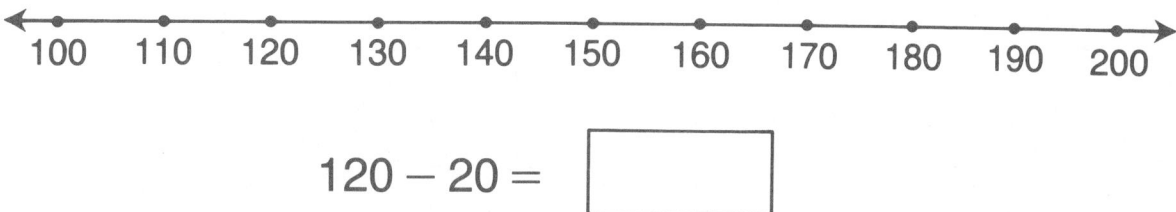

120 − 20 = [100]

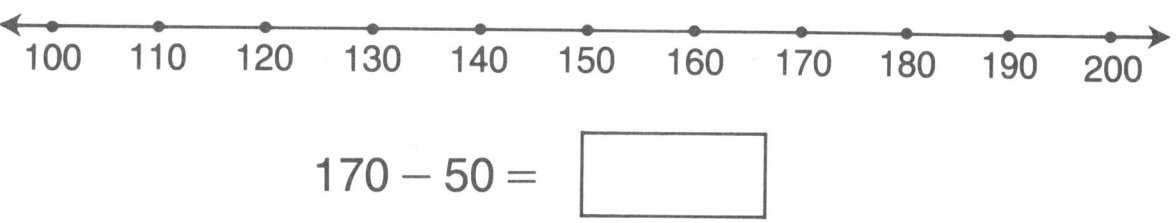

170 − 50 = [120]

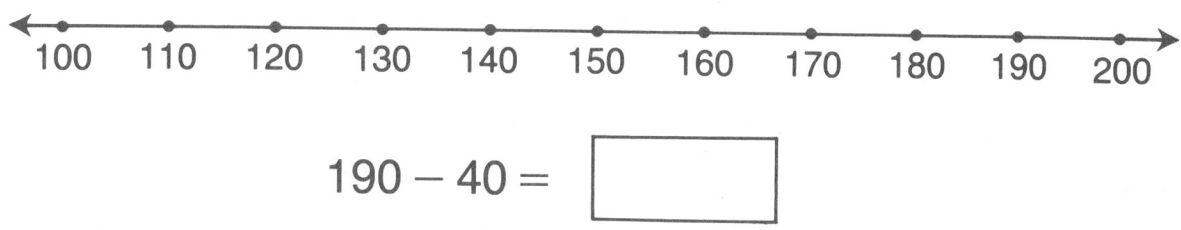

190 − 40 = [150]

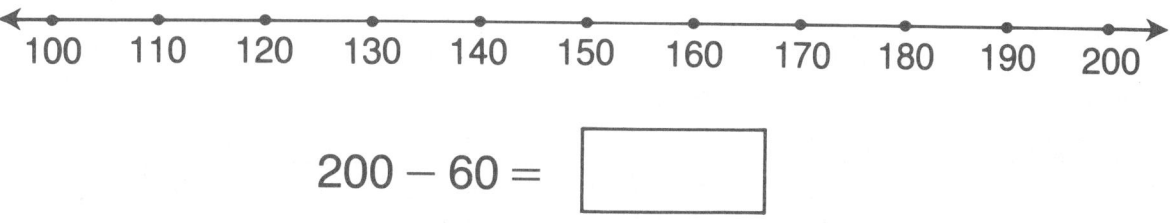

200 − 60 = [140]

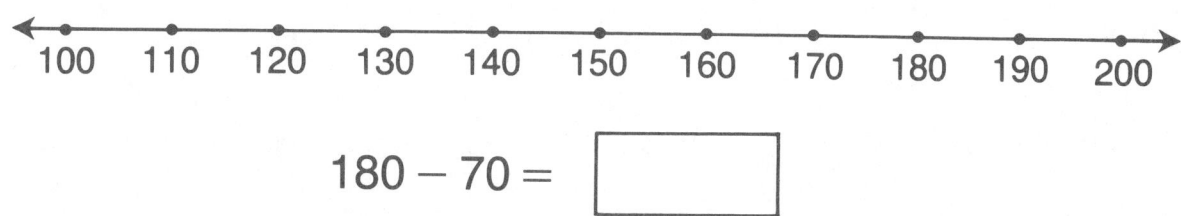

180 − 70 = [110]

34   Write the answers.

Add 1 to each of these numbers:

2 [ ]   30 [ ]   49 [ ]   180 [ ]

9 [ ]   19 [ ]   149 [ ]   199 [ ]

Subtract 1 from each of these numbers:

7 [ ]   40 [ ]   101 [ ]   141 [ ]

4 [ ]   11 [ ]   90 [ ]   190 [ ]

Add 10 to each of these numbers:

8 [ ]   19 [ ]   55 [ ]   155 [ ]

1 [ ]   30 [ ]   70 [ ]   170 [ ]

Subtract 10 from each of these numbers:

19 [ ]   12 [ ]   100 [ ]   120 [ ]

36 [ ]   20 [ ]   136 [ ]   200 [ ]

Which is greater?

13 or 31 [ ]   43 or 34 [ ]   200 or 165 [ ]

21 or 12 [ ]   24 or 42 [ ]   108 or 180 [ ]

Write the missing numerals.   35

10 20 30 40 50 60 ◇ 80

30 40 ◇ 60 70 80 90 ◇

70 ◇ 90 ◇ 110 120 130 140

◇ 100 110 120 ◇ ◇ 150 160

130 ◇ 150 ◇ 170 180 ◇ ◇

90 80 70 60 50 ◇ 30 20

120 110 100 ◇ 80 70 60 ◇

◇ 140 130 120 110 ◇ 90 80

170 160 ◇ 140 130 120 ◇ ◇

200 ◇ 180 ◇ 160 ◇ 140 ◇

36   Write the values of the missing coins.

3p = (1p) + (1p) + ◯	4p = (1p) + (1p) + ◯
5p = (2p) + (2p) + ◯	6p = (2p) + (2p) + ◯
7p = (1p) + (1p) + ◯	8p = (5p) + (2p) + ◯
9p = (5p) + (2p) + ◯	11p = (1p) + (5p) + ◯
12p = (2p) + (5p) + ◯	12p = (1p) + (1p) + ◯
13p = (1p) + (2p) + ◯	14p = (2p) + (10p) + ◯
15p = (5p) + (5p) + ◯	16p = (1p) + (5p) + ◯
17p = (5p) + (2p) + ◯	20p = (5p) + (10p) + ◯
21p = (10p) + (10p) + ◯	22p = (10p) + (10p) + ◯
25p = (10p) + (10p) + ◯	30p = (10p) + (10p) + ◯

Write the values of the missing coins.　　37

40p = (10p) + (10p) + (10p) + ( )

54p = (50p) + (2p) + (1p) + ( )

58p = (50p) + (5p) + (2p) + ( )

65p = (50p) + (5p) + (5p) + ( )

67p = (50p) + (10p) + (5p) + ( )

70p = (50p) + (5p) + (5p) + (5p) + ( )

72p = (50p) + (10p) + (10p) + (1p) + ( )

74p = (50p) + (10p) + (10p) + (2p) + ( )

82p = (50p) + (10p) + (10p) + (10p) + ( )

85p = (50p) + (10p) + (10p) + (10p) + ( )

38   Write the names of the shapes.

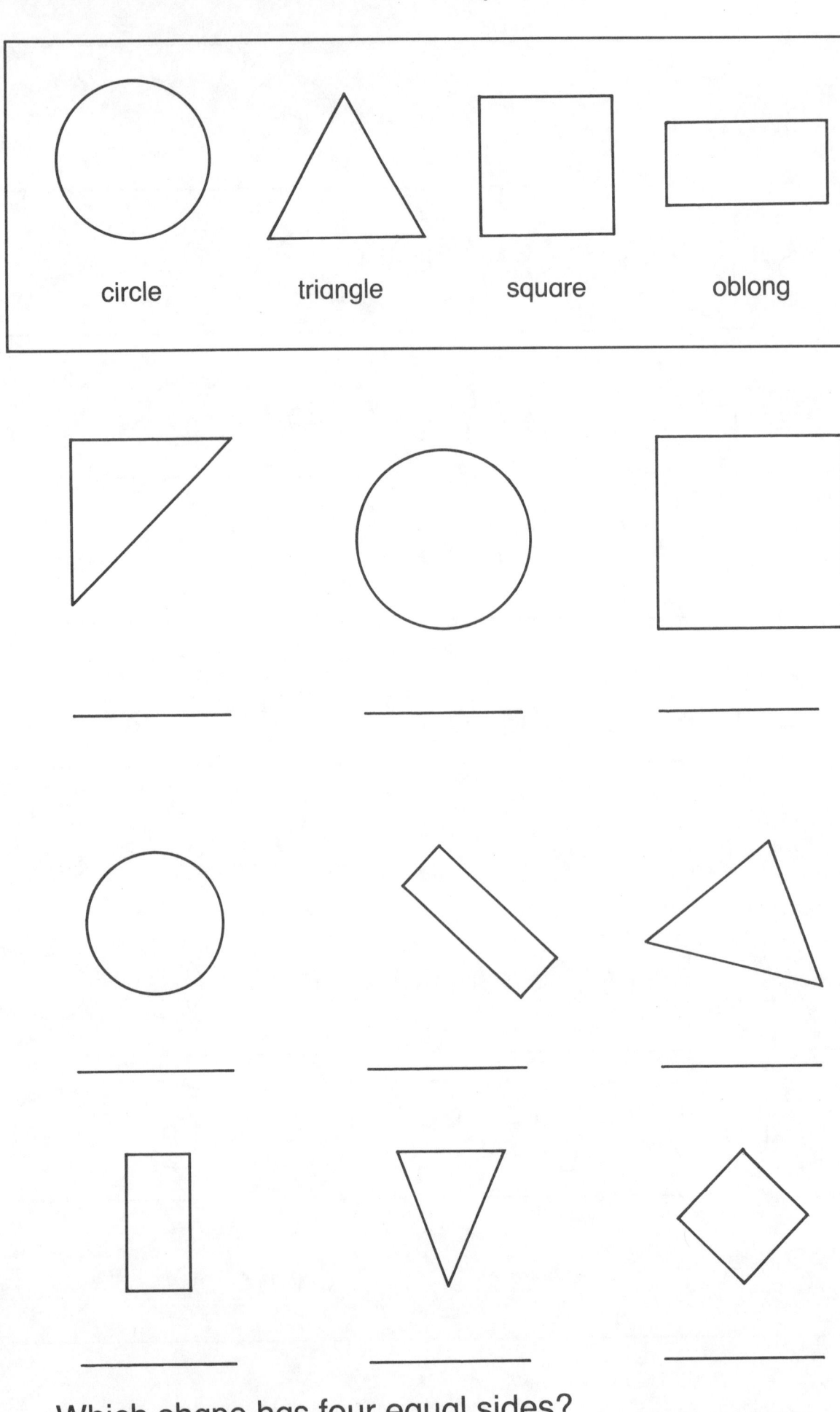

Which shape has four equal sides? _____
Which shape has three sides? _____

Colour the shapes mentioned. 39

Colour the circles.

Colour the triangles.

Colour the squares.

Colour the oblongs.

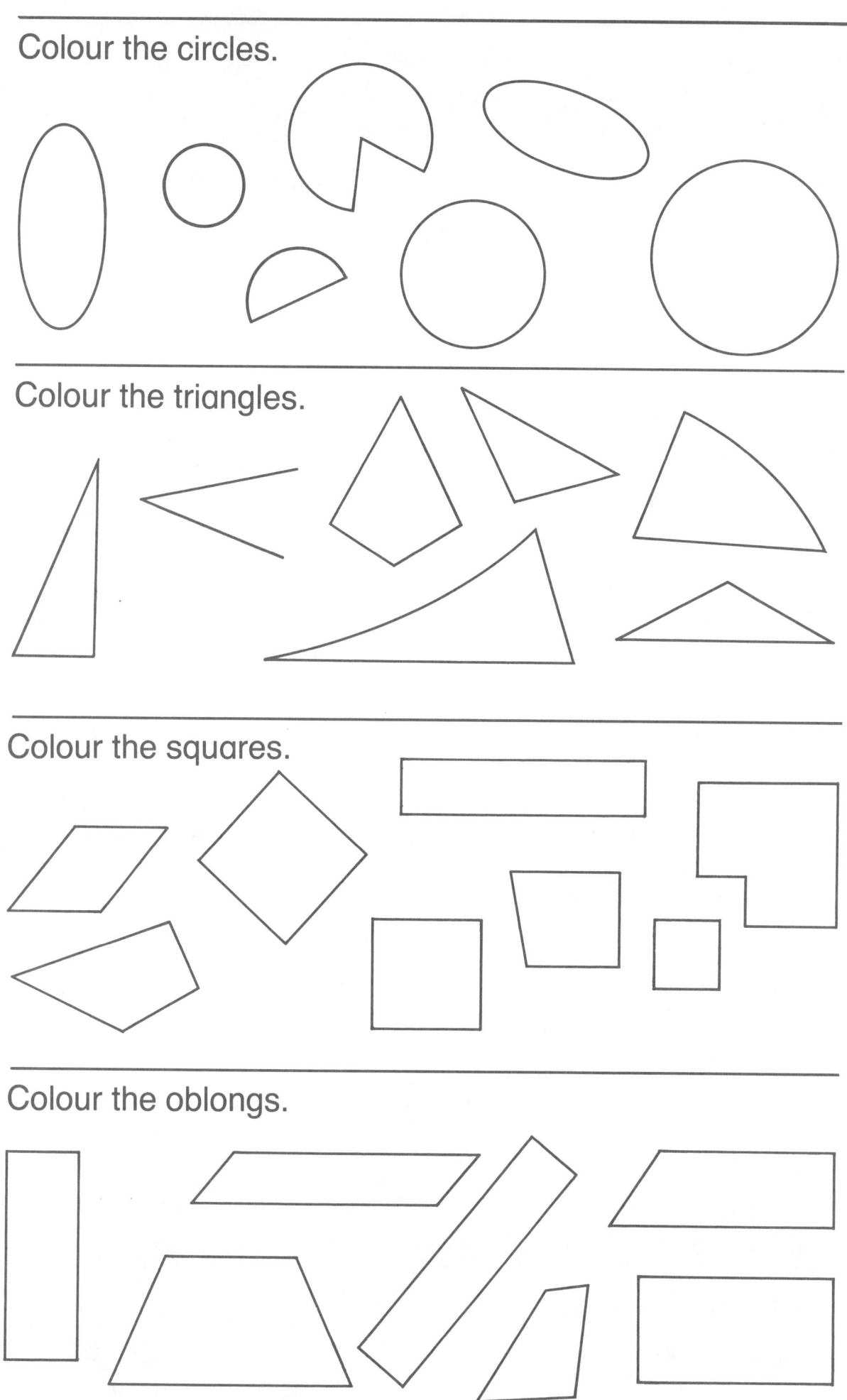

40 Days of the week.

Here are the names of the days of the week:

| Sunday | Monday | Tuesday | Wednesday |
| Thursday | Friday | Saturday | |

Now finish these:

Sun. is short for _____

Mon. is short for _____

Tue. is short for _____

Wed. is short for _____

Thu. is short for _____

Fri. is short for _____

Sat. is short for _____

The day before Wednesday is _____

The day before Thursday is _____

The day after Sunday is _____

The day after Thursday is _____

The day before Friday is _____

The day before Sunday is _____

The day after Saturday is _____

Which day comes

between Thursday and Saturday? _____

between Monday and Wednesday? _____

between Tuesday and Thursday? _____

between Sunday and Tuesday? _____

between Wednesday and Friday? _____

between Saturday and Monday? _____

between Friday and Sunday? _____

Months of the year.   41

Here are the names of the months of the year:

January	February	March	April
May	June	July	August
September	October	November	December

Now finish these:

The 1st month is called _____

The 2nd month is called _____

The 3rd month is called _____

The 4th month is called _____

The 5th month is called _____

The 6th month is called _____

The 7th month is called _____

The 8th month is called _____

The 9th month is called _____

The 10th month is called _____

The 11th month is called _____

The 12th month is called _____

Dates are sometimes written in figures.

   3 9 82 means the 3rd day of September 1982.

  26 2 82 means the 26th day of _____

  12 12 82 means the 12th day of _____

  28 8 82 means the 28th day of _____

   7 1 82 means the 7th day of _____

  30 6 82 means the 30th day of _____

  14 4 82 means the 14th day of _____

   9 10 82 means the 9th day of _____

  15 7 82 means the 15th day of _____

42 Draw the hands to show the times given.

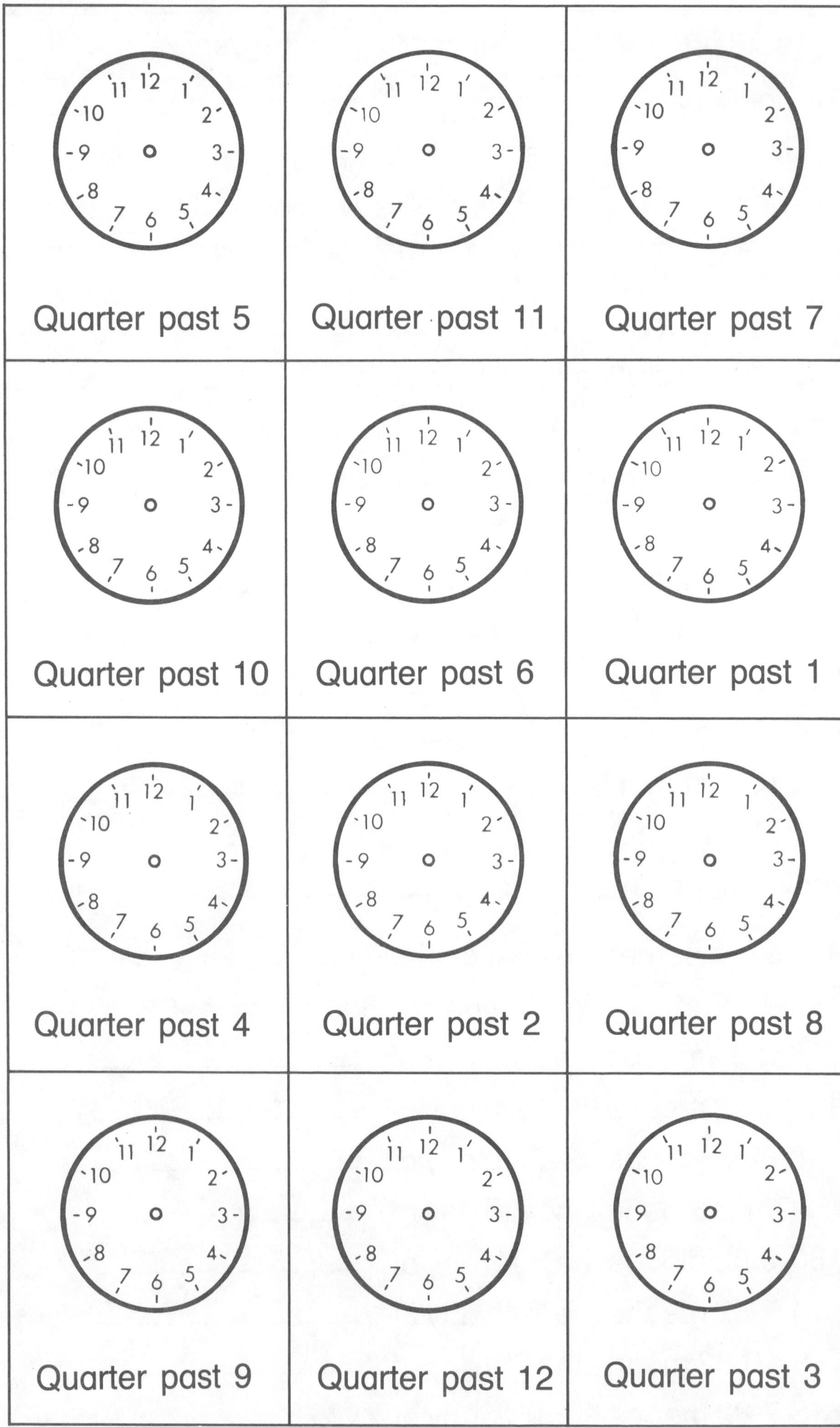

Draw the hands to show the times given. 43

Quarter to 2	Quarter to 6	Quarter to 11
Quarter to 1	Quarter to 8	Quarter to 3
Quarter to 7	Quarter to 5	Quarter to 12
Quarter to 10	Quarter to 4	Quarter to 9

44 True or False?
Draw a ring round the right word.

19 is one less than 20	(True)	False
50 is one more than 40	True	(False)
5 + 7 = 7 + 5	True	False
16 − 10 = 10 − 16	True	False
26 + 4 = 30	True	False
126 + 4 = 130	True	False
19 + 8 = 198	True	False
123 = 12 + 3	True	False
200 = 100 + 100	True	False
5 + 5 + 5 = 20	True	False
70 − 10 = 7	True	False
140 − 40 = 100	True	False
60 + 30 = 30	True	False
100 − 50 = fifty	True	False
160 + 40 = two hundred	True	False
4 + 5 + 7 = 7 + 4 + 5	True	False